JASCHA HEIFETZ

Transcriptions For Violin
From
George Gershwin's
PORGY AND BESS

CONTENTS

chappell/intersong
music group—usa

Exclusively Distributed By

HAL•LEONARD®
CORPORATION
7777 W. BLUEMOUND RD. P.O. BOX 13819 MILWAUKEE, WI 53213

PORGY AND BESS

George Gershwin (1898-1937) is one of the most beloved and influential composers of the 20th Century. He possessed a rare talent of being able to write both popular songs and more "serious" music for the concert stage, and in all his musical ventures retained a distinctive, original style that was definitely "Gershwin".

Porgy and Bess seems to have had a special place in Gershwin's heart. It certainly is his longest and most ambitious composition, lasting well over three hours in its complete form. At the time of the premiere (Alvin Theatre, New York, October 10, 1935) *Porgy and Bess* was such an original creation that some people were not sure what to make of it. Was it a Broadway show? Who had ever heard of a Broadway show with such an expansive score? Was it an opera? Who expected an opera to contain "popular" songs?

The show was obviously well ahead of its time, and was not a success in that first production, although many of the songs became immediately famous. Some criticized it as being merely a collection of hit songs rather than a true opera. However, others praised it as the beginning of a new, important folk-opera genre. *Porgy and Bess* gained in popularity, and at last achieved fame and success on stage in an extensive world tour in the 1950s. Since that time there have been several revivals of the show on Broadway, a film version, instrumental arrangements, and the show's unquestioned acceptance in the repertory of the world's major opera companies.

These arrangements for violin and piano combine the immortal songs of Gershwin with the classic purity of one of the world's greatest musicians, Jascha Heifetz. This rare combination can only enhance the beauty and versatility of songs that have already found their place in the hearts of so many.

Jascha Heifetz

The name Jascha Heifetz is synonymous with virtuoso violin playing. The Russian-born prodigy began violin studies at the age of three with his father, Ruvim Heifetz, a professional violinist. By the age of six the young Heifetz was able to perform Mendelssohn's *Violin Concerto*. He was admitted to the St. Petersburg Conservatory in 1910, soon to study directly under Leopold Auer, the renowned violinist and pedagogue. On May 23, 1912 the 11-year old Heifetz made a sensational debut in Berlin, leading to his performance of Tchaikovsky's *Violin Concerto* with the Berlin Philharmonic Orchestra later the same year. In 1917 he left his native Russia to tour the U.S.A., and gave a triumphant Carnegie Hall debut on October 27. Jascha Heifetz became an American citizen in 1925.

Early performances, including those in England (1920), Australia (1921), the Far East (1923), Palestine (1926), and Russia (1934) left an indelible mark on the world of classical violin playing. In addition to unparalleled technical virtuosity, Heifetz's performances displayed a powerful, radiant tone, always guided by exquisite taste and classical purity.

"Summertime" and
"A Woman is a Sometime Thing"
(from "Porgy and Bess")

Words by Debose Heyward & Ira Gershwin
Music by George Gershwin

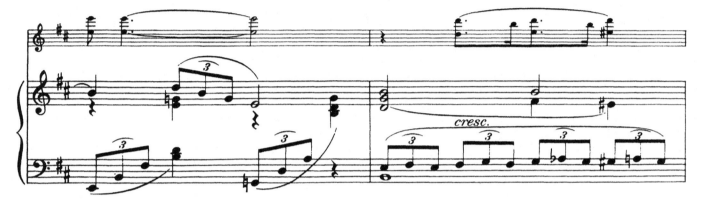

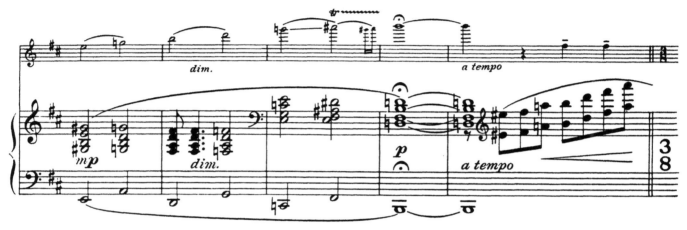

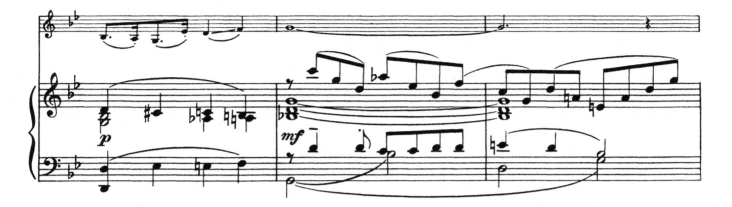

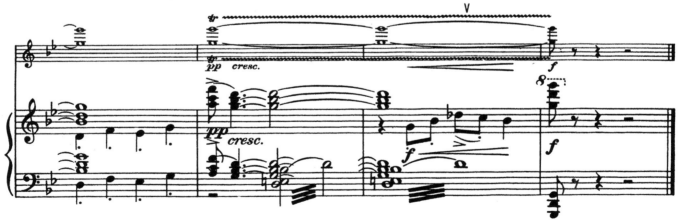

Harbor Island, California.
Nov. 7, 1944

My Man's Gone Now
(from "Porgy and Bess")

Words by Debose Heyward & Ira Gershwin
Music by George Gershwin

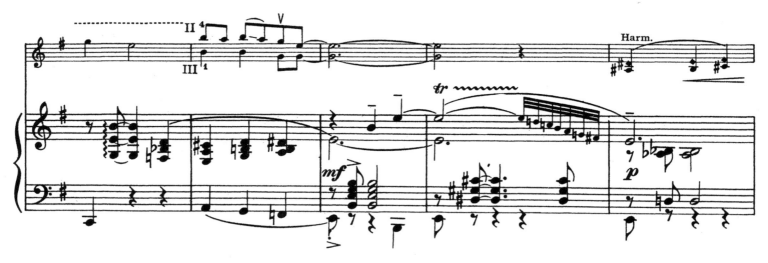

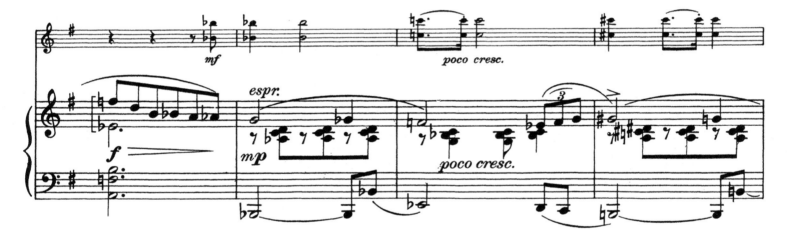

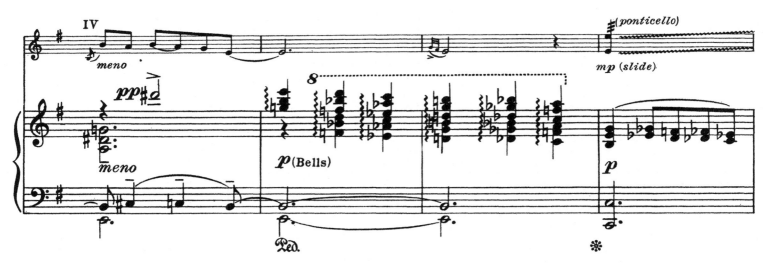

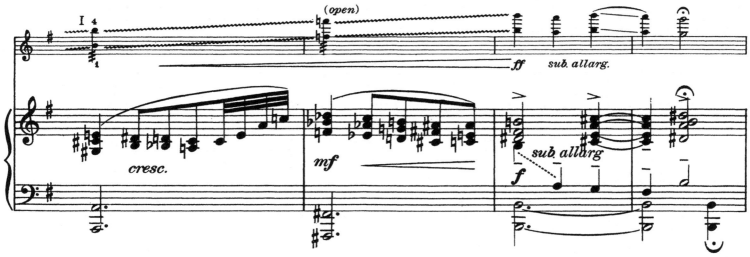

Harbor Island,
California.
Nov. 12, 1944.

JASCHA HEIFETZ

Transcriptions For Violin
From
George Gershwin's

PORGY AND BESS

Summertime / A Woman Is A Sometime Thing
My Man's Gone Now
Bess, You Is My Woman Now
It Ain't Necessarily So
Tempo di Blues

music group—usa

EXCLUSIVELY DISTRIBUTED BY

7777 W. BLUEMOUND RD. P.O. BOX 13819 MILWAUKEE, WI 53213

"Summertime" and
"A Woman is a Sometime Thing"
(from "Porgy and Bess")

Violin

Words by Debose Heyward & Ira Gershwin
Music by George Gershwin

Harbor Island, California.
Nov. 7, 1944

My Man's Gone Now
(from "Porgy and Bess")

Violin

Words by Debose Heyward & Ira Gershwin
Music by George Gershwin

Violin

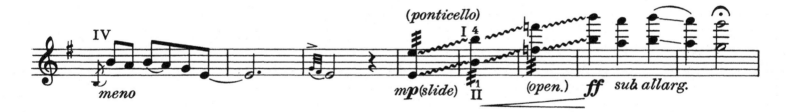

Harbor Island, California.
Nov. 12, 1944.

Bess, You Is My Woman Now

(from "Porgy and Bess")

Violin

Words by Dubose Heyward & Ira Gershwin
Music by George Gershwin

*A cut may be made from this sign to the next asterik

Harbor Island, Calif.
Nov. 5, 1944

It Ain't Necessarily So
(from "Porgy and Bess")

Words by Dubose Heyward & Ira Gershwin
Music by George Gershwin

Violin

* Approx. to B♮ - without reaching any *particular* note.

Harbor Island, California.
Oct. 30, 1944

Tempo di Blues

Based on "Picnics is alright" and "There's a boat dat's leavin' soon for New York"

(from **"Porgy and Bess"**)

Violin

Words by Debose Heyward & Ira Gershwin
Music by George Gershwin

Violin

Harbor Island, California.
Oct. 29, 1944.

Bess, You Is My Woman Now

(from "Porgy and Bess")

Words by Dubose Heyward & Ira Gershwin
Music by George Gershwin

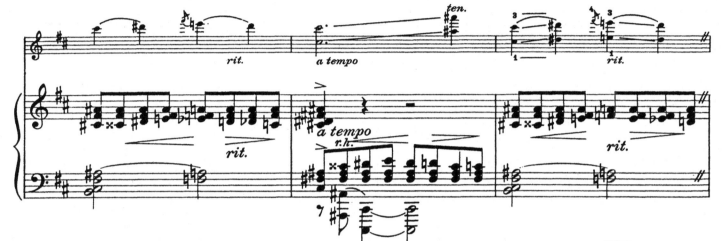

Poco sostenuto

* A cut may be made from this sign to the next asterik on page 7

Harbor Island, Calif.
Nov. 5, 1944

It Ain't Necessarily So
(from "Porgy and Bess")

Words by Dubose Heyward & Ira Gershwin
Music by George Gershwin

Allegro

Dance
Tempo I°

* Approx. to B♮ - without reaching any *particular* note.

Harbor Island, California.
Oct. 30, 1944

Tempo di Blues

Based on "Picnics is alright" and "There's a boat dat's leavin' soon for New York"

(from "Porgy and Bess")

Words by Debose Heyward & Ira Gershwin
Music by George Gershwin

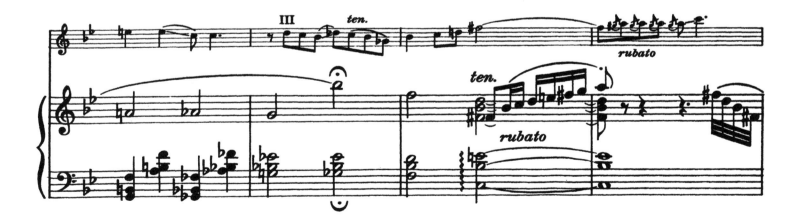

Moderato (♩=96) ("There's a boat dat's leavin' soon for New York")

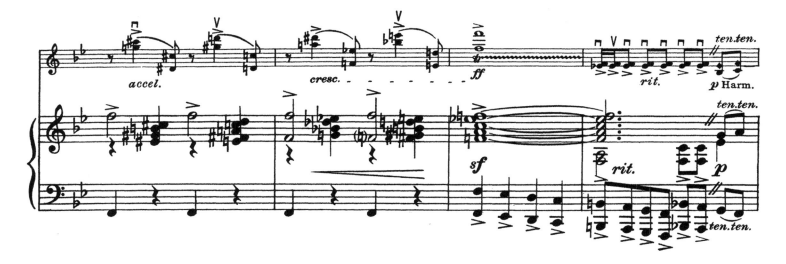

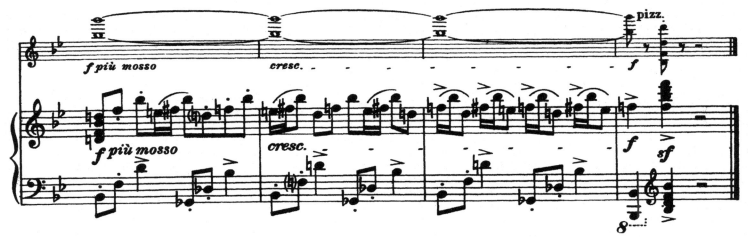

Harbor Island, California.
Oct. 29, 1944.